PRAISE FOR
Investing in Life

"I was interested in investing in real estate for a long time. I was frequently listening to real estate podcasts and reading articles about the benefits of real estate investing. But I was hesitant in investing because I frankly didn't know enough and didn't know who to trust to take the big step. But David, who has been my colleague in pediatric dentistry for over ten years, has been a wise guide and mentor in multifamily syndication investing. I have invested with David in seven real estate syndication deals as of today and I hope to keep on investing with him and to grow my passive income portfolio."

JAEPIL KIM DDS

Pediatric Dentist

"An honest story of his journey into Multifamily Real Estate from a man who just wants to help and inspire those around him."

KEVIN DEAN, CFA

Principal - RockBridge Investment Group

"David is one of the most generous, kindhearted, energetic individuals you will ever meet. His vision and drive combine to make him one of the most influential people we've had the pleasure of working with. Not only is he selfless and caring, he also has a business mindset and can problem solve quickly in order for the team to excel, no matter what role he is playing at the time. To know David is to laugh and know joy, all while rolling your sleeves up to get the task done!"

JON AND SAM WELLS

"In the 12 years I have known David, he has been an accomplished pediatric dentist and business owner, a fierce semi-pro athlete, a devoted father and husband, and a generous friend. He has an incomparable tenacity and passion for life. I am convinced he has the determination to make anything possible and successful."

ALLISON BRICKER-WOOLPERT CRNA, MSN, BSN, RN

"First of all, David is a fantastic human being, family man, and friend. Second, he's a sharp, driven, and savvy investor. He's the kind of guy that, if you're lucky enough to find, you'll want to ride his coattails. He'll take you places if you're ready."

POWELL CHEE
Founder, Radiant Storage

"When I met Dr. David Iglewicz, he told me about his multiunit real estate investment vision, and I was quite intrigued. He was modest and realistic with what the returns would be. Having been burned by a few different opportunities in the past decade, I was hesitant but felt there was a lot of wisdom in this investment strategy. I started with one property to see how it went, and was immediately encouraged by the regular property reports, transparency of operations, cash flows, and the distributions I received. Listening and seeing the due diligence David's team was putting into each exploration is affirming and encouraging. There's a reason their deals perform well, and it's because of their specific and well-vetted research processes. I anxiously look forward to Dr. Iglewicz's next property purchase and confidently invest in each opportunity he brings. I still place some investments in higher risk and higher return opportunities. But my desire is to swing less for the fences and stay disciplined in the wisdom of real estate assets, their physical holding, and of course the predictable distributions each quarter. Thanks Doc! I'm grateful to be along for the opportunities you and your team presents."

DAVID T. EVANS DMD, FAAPD

"Working with David has been like winning the Real Estate Investing lottery. He's not only a top expert in multifamily investing but also has the years of experience that brings true stability to your investments. It's a bonus that he's also a really great guy to be around."

HETHIR RODRIQUEZ
Entrepreneur, MF Investor

"I love the idea of being involved with successful people from the start so I can learn and profit from them. I love the idea of multifamily. I wouldn't know where to start and wouldn't have the confidence to be involved in multifamily without being able to work with knowledgeable people that have successfully done this for years."

SEAN SCHEXNAYDER DMD

Pediatric Dentist

INVESTING IN

LIFE

Creating Financial Freedom through Multifamily Real Estate

INVESTING IN

LIFE

Creating Financial Freedom through Multifamily Real Estate

DAVID IGLEWICZ, DMD

Advantage

Published by Advantage, Charleston, South Carolina.
Member of Advantage Media.

ADVANTAGE is a registered trademark, and the Advantage colophon is a trademark of Advantage Media Group, Inc.

Printed in the United States of America.

10 9 8 7 6 5 4 3 2 1

ISBN: 978-1-64225-397-9 (Paperback)
ISBN: 978-1-64225-419-8 (eBook)

LCCN: 2022914458

Book design by Amanda Haskin.

This publication is designed to provide accurate and authoritative information in regard to the subject matter covered. It is sold with the understanding that the publisher is not engaged in rendering legal, accounting, or other professional services. If legal advice or other expert assistance is required, the services of a competent professional person should be sought.

Advantage Media helps busy entrepreneurs, CEOs, and leaders write and publish a book to grow their business and become the authority in their field. Advantage authors comprise an exclusive community of industry professionals, idea-makers, and thought leaders. Do you have a book idea or manuscript for consideration? We would love to hear from you at **AdvantageMedia.com**.

I want to thank my wife Sandy who opened the doors to my feelings, helped me to think bigger, and showed unconditional love. Thank you for allowing me to grow!

Thank you to my children Brandon and Sydney who every day inspire me to do a little bit more.

Thanks to my dad who always had this magical spark and believed in me; my mom whose outgoing nature was a model to follow; and my sister who every day uses her skills to help others.

Joey, Chris, Sherlock, Marc, Brandon, Sam, Jonathan, Kevin, Dave, Matt, Justin, and many more are a wonderful circle of friends and partners.

I want to thank the coaches who have changed my life: Rod, Faisal, Dr. Sean, Powell, Del, and many more.

Thank you to the multiple dental teams that I get to work with.

And I want to thank every investor who left the standard stocks and bonds and made the leap into Multifamily Investing. I visualized your success for a long time, and I love to see your wealth grow.

Contents

PART ONE

How It All Started

What if you could invest in a way that both grows your wealth and also invests in the lives of others? What if you could break out of the meaningless cycle of traditional investing and enjoy steady growth that requires very little work—or stress—on your part?

Believe me, I know it sounds too good to be true. Maybe it even sounds like a cheesy sales pitch. But really, I ask these questions to be the start of a conversation, and like any conversation, it's going to bounce around a bit. I've never been diagnosed with ADHD, but if I was, they'd probably throw in a few extra Ds for good measure. Because I want to talk about two things here that don't seem like they're connected: being a dentist and what it looks like to invest in multifamily real estate.

Don't worry. I'm not going to go into my entire life story. This isn't really that kind of book. But I do want to explain how the course of my career as a pediatric dentist led me to starting up my own multifamily-unit real estate company, Prostoig Capital, and, most importantly, how doing so has helped me find joy and purpose by helping others in a unique way that also increases my confidence in my financial future.

I swear I didn't set out to become some kind of real estate guru; it's just the direction that life has taken me, and I'm incredibly grateful it did. And maybe I'm getting ahead of myself a bit, but when I really sat down to think about it, my journey to multifamily-unit real estate was a long time coming.

In fact, it started years ago when I was still just a teenager. My dad was a statistician at Temple University, and one day he came home from work and started speaking to me in his characteristic Russian accent.

"David, you won't believe it," he started.

"What?" I asked.

"Today, I found out one of my students—a C student, not even a very great student—is now a multimillionaire."

Obviously, this caught my attention. "How?" I asked.

In his disbelief, my dad replied, "Well, turns out he got involved in real estate—multifamily real estate—and he got lucky. That's how."

Here's the thing, though: I don't think you can just "get lucky," especially not in real estate. That's just not how it works. As an educator, I think my dad just couldn't accept that someone could be unsuccessful in academia but successful financially. So that moment always stuck with me, in the back of my head, as a possibility that I could always look into.

But I also didn't originally set out to be a dentist either. At the end of the day, I really just always wanted to be happy and bring happiness to others. So how did I end up in dentistry?

In high school, I was really into biology and chemistry. The truth is that I really wanted to be a waste-management engineer at the time. I wanted to develop bacteria that could safely dissolve garbage bags and help the environment.

But I also used to like making model airplanes and rockets when I was a kid, and I was really interested in the gadgets and tools I saw at my own dentist's office. So I started hanging out with him to learn more about all these cool tools, and then after my first couple of years of college, I said, "You know what? I think I'm going to become a dentist."

Before I knew it, I was in dental school and hanging out with the

> **At the end of the day, I really just always wanted to be happy and bring happiness to others.**

pediatric dentists—not so much for the kids, actually, but because I really liked the personality the pediatric dentists had. They were warm and caring, and I just enjoyed being around them. They said, "David, you're naturally a kid. Why don't you help take care of kids too?"

Upon graduating residency, my plan was to start up my own practice. But then I got a call from an established pediatric dentist, who was battling leukemia at the time, and he let me know that his son was going to be taking over his practice but needed a partner. I met up with him to hear him out, and he said, "Why don't you work for me part time, meet my son, and see if the two of you get along?" And since it's very rare for me to meet somebody who I don't get along with, it was pretty easy to agree to.

This was around 2002, and I was moonlighting for that office. Then a year later, I joined the practice as a full-time associate. After the father passed away, I was brought on as an associate partner, and the son and I agreed to open up a practice together and go fifty-fifty on it. Long story short, we ended up doing better than I expected, and I started asking myself, "How do I make this income grow?"

I don't think I'm alone in this thought. When you've been a medical professional for a while and built up a solid business, it's only natural to think about how to grow your wealth outside of your practice. And you should! You never want to have all your eggs in one basket, right? If you're like me, you want to build wealth not just for yourself but for your family or for charity.

Maybe, like me, you're fed up or frustrated with the standard financial advice of chasing fluctuating stock numbers, halfheartedly day-trading, and acting out of fear— selling when the market goes down and buying when it goes up. That's where I found myself not too long ago, playing a mental game driven by fear, leaving me fatigued by financial FOMO—until I started asking myself some questions:

→ "Why does everyone think investing in the stock market is a safe investment?"

→ "Is there a way I can invest that will also give me a sense of purpose?"

The first red flag I noticed about traditional investing happened back when I was still in dental school. I had friends who were a little ahead of me in the program, and some of them were investing in new technology companies and were putting in $1,000 or $2,000 into them and then making $10,000 overnight from an IPO. I thought this looked really promising for myself, but—this was right around the year 2000—then the dot-com bubble burst happened, and I saw them lose all that money they had in the tech companies. And unfortunately, many of them had been doing this using loan money, so now they'd lost it all and didn't have any way to pay their living expenses, which meant that they now had to start working on top of their school responsibilities. Turns out, I'd dodged a bullet by not following their lead, and it taught me early on that there's no such thing as a "sure thing" when investing in the market.

So I started with all of the traditional things, like a 401(k). But then the second red flag that came along was in 2008 when the housing market crashed, and I saw that a 401(k) became more like a 201(k)—literally, my balance was cut in half. Thanks to my statistician dad, I've always been comfortable around numbers, and I thought the numbers couldn't be right and brought it up to my advisor, saying, "Hey, isn't there something wrong with these numbers?"

But what really shook me up about that whole situation was when I went to a dental meeting around this time. Here I was in my early thirties, upset about the losses in my 401(k), and then in walked some older dentists in their seventies, pale as ghosts, hands trembling both from age and from fear. Because here they were, having to go back to work because they had just lost most of their retirement savings.

I said to myself, "I can't let that happen to me."

Still, it took me a while to learn how to do things different. I thought, "Maybe if I take more of a hands-on approach with my money, then I'll feel more in control." So around 2010, I was managing my own stocks and investing on my own, constantly checking the numbers and making trades to make a buck here and there. Basically, I was trying to be a part-time day trader when I was in between patients. While this made me feel more in control of the outcome, it didn't bring me any sense of fulfillment or purpose with how I was using my money. Sure, I was still serving one patient at a time in my office, but there was no greater meaning or impact to how I was growing my money.

Plus, it just wasn't that profitable. I realized, at one point, that I had spent probably five hundred hours of day-trading to make five hundred bucks. It was a lot of work, a bit of random luck, and—c'mon, let's be honest—not that great a payoff when you consider I'd made about a dollar an hour and went through a lot of unnecessary stress.

Then, in 2015, the real wake-up call happened for me while I was walking on the beach with my dad. He'd been sick for a while and had gone through several quadruple bypasses, always fighting through them because he was a man of strength, power, and warm kindness. But as we were walking along, he was looking jaundiced and put his arm around me, saying, "David, I'm really proud of you."

And as good as it felt for him to say this to me, it also made me feel bad because I didn't feel proud of myself. On the outside, I can always appear to be very optimistic and energetic, but on the inside at that point, I was going through a lot of turmoil because I felt disconnected from who I was and what my purpose should be.

On the outside, I was making lots of money. But you know what they say: "Money can't buy happiness." And, man, did I suddenly realize how true that was. So it was hard for me to hear my dad say how proud of me he was when, on the inside, I wasn't sure what there was to be proud about. I felt like I needed a mission, something that was going to guide me—and something that wasn't based on "luck," which I don't really believe in anyway.

Burned out by my little day-trading stint, I started looking for new creative ways to increase my income outside of dentistry. I wasn't trying to do anything "different"; I was just looking for the best use of my money and time to increase wealth.

I finally accepted the hard truth that all investing requires some level of risk. But I was so fed up with what I'd been trying and with the lack of purpose I was feeling that I was open to trying something new and treating myself as a bit of a test subject in the process. Because whatever I ended up doing, I didn't want it to just be for myself—I wanted to find something that could help others like me.

My mind went back to seeing those aging dentists in 2008 having to go back to work after they had put so much trust in what their financial advisors had told them. I'm not trying to bad-mouth all financial advisors—I'm sure they meant well—but I had an ethical concern with how that industry was doing things at the time, continuing to take percentages of what was left even though their actions had contributed to what had been lost.

So I wanted to prevent that same thing happening to others and help dentists like me find a better way. That was my real motivation—and it still is—because it wasn't just about making money and helping others find financial freedom but about them feeling happy about how their money is being used, not to line the pockets of Wall Street fat cats but to make a difference to families we serve every day in our offices.

At the time, I was still a minority partner in the dental office. Since my partner was an entrepreneurial type and dentistry was hot at the time, he bought more and more dental offices. I brought up the idea of private equity to him, which he ended up being a big fan of, and we decided to sell the practice in 2016. This meant I got a big payout, but then, all of a sudden, I was scared instead of relieved. Now that I had this big chunk of cash, I realized I had to protect it.

And even though I had entrusted this money to my financial advisor, I didn't really trust what was happening with it. I was constantly stressing out about it—checking how the stocks and bonds were doing, double-checking all the fees on the work he was doing—and I just felt wrong about the whole thing. I was supposed to be paying him to take care of things, but my actions showed I clearly didn't trust him.

That's when I finally remembered, from all those years before, the idea of multifamily real estate and my dad's student who had invested in it. For one thing, the numbers behind how the business worked made sense to me, but also the purpose behind it clicked with me and my personality. Anyone who knows me knows that I love to be happy and love to get others excited and happy—and the idea of multifamily units really got me excited. I'd noticed that many of the patients I was seeing in pediatric dentistry were just like the people living in these apartment buildings. What if I could play a role in improving their living situation?

I know this is an incredibly obvious statement, but dentistry is an intimate business—any medical profession is. But so is working with people living in apartments; it requires the same kind of communication and the same kind of care. So it was like a light bulb went off for me. This was my mission. I could help lots of families by providing them with a good place to live, invite other dentists to invest in the opportunity, and make money together from it while also doing right by those families.

But I knew that if I was going to do it right and help others in the process, I needed to learn it inside and out. The first major misconception I had was that I thought I could do everything myself. Now, I knew it wasn't going to be as easy as just walking into a bank and saying "Hi, I'd like to buy an apartment building, please," but I had no idea how much hard work it was going to be.

In 2016, I started looking into how it all worked and soon found myself overloaded with conference calls, which I was trying to fit around seeing patients at my new practice, and also trying to be a professional bike racer (that's a whole other story, though). Long story short, I was doing too much at once and not spending enough time where it really mattered—with my amazing family.

But I don't give up easily, so even though I was really struggling to find properties that met my criteria, I tried to do a couple of deals on my own. Looking back at that time, I realize now that I was trying to escape—from problems at the practice, family problems, stress—but I was just making it worse by trying to do it all on my own. So the first big lesson I learned was that if you're going to do this, then you need to do it with other people. You need to have great partners to share the load with you.

So, in 2019, I finally said to myself, "You know what? I'm going to start out investing in other people's deals instead and learn from them." So I started out by becoming an investor myself in another multifamily real estate company. And now I had to confront what had been one of my biggest fears in the learning process—wiring money. For one thing, I'd never wired money before in my life. And when you invest in multifamily real estate, well, you're going to end up having to wire a significant amount of money—$25,000 or $200,000 or maybe even a million depending on the deal and how much you're wanting to contribute to it. And that first time was scary, but then I realized that even in traditional investing, these same kinds of money transfers are happening all the time. You just don't see it happening. Once I accepted that, it didn't feel so scary.

To get some balance back in my life, I started off as a passive investor and ended up doing several deals that way. I learned how one of the great things about this kind of investing is that you can be as involved—or uninvolved—as you want to be. It turned out that I wasn't the only "passive" investor in the group, which helped me overcome some fear about the whole process because I wasn't doing it solo—I was joining up with other dentists just like me as a minority partner and learning the business from the bottom up.

As I learned more about the business and saw the benefits that I was getting from it, both in helping people and in generating wealth, I realized that the deals I was going after were too small. So the next thing I learned was that the smaller deals were actually riskier than the bigger deals. I know that sounds wrong, but the fact is that the bigger the deal is, the more likely it is the banks will help you out because they don't want it to fail. Whereas with the smaller ones, well, they don't care if those fail because if things go south, then they'll just take them over from you anyway.

Then I stepped up my involvement until I was interested in buying a property for myself, running it, and building a team. But my biggest concern was for other investors. I wanted to make sure that if I was going to ask someone to come partner with me and invest in multifamily units, then I needed to be able to add value to them as part of the process.

For me, it wasn't just about learning the process of buying and running the property, the nuts and bolts of it, but structuring the deals with an investor-first mindset.

So then I signed up for a coaching and mentorship program, which helped me get connected with more like-minded people. I attended a conference where I found others who were willing to take on a lot of risk—and were excited about it. It got me amped up and raised my own excitement to the point that I said to myself, "I need to do this now."

My wife, Sandy, has always been my biggest fan and supporter in all this. She also went to dental school and has practiced some, but really she's had the hardest job of raising our two amazing kids, Brandon and Sydney. We first met around 1996 because she liked Freud, my golden retriever. I liked her already, but it took the dog for her to start liking me—talk about man's best friend.

We married in 2000 and moved to the Philadelphia area, and she supported us while I was in dental school. Given our long history, one of the greatest confirmations I've had that I'm doing the right thing is when she's told me how she loves the way that doing real estate has energized me and brought me a new sense of purpose beyond dentistry or biking or anything else I've ever tried.

Speaking of biking, a final wake-up call for me happened in October of 2019 while I was in England to race my bike at a world championship. But after I didn't get past the qualifying round, I found myself sitting on the hotel room floor, thinking about how I was away from my family, missing my daughter's birthday, and thinking, "What am I doing? Yeah, it's cool to be in England, but what am I getting out of this? Who am I helping with all this bike racing?" I realized I'd spent a ton of time and money on something that was just an escape, when I now had something right in front of me that I was also passionate about and could help other dentists and medical professionals.

Even though I'd lost the race, I actually had a smile on my face, because that's when I really committed to everything I had been learning up to that point. That's when I decided that if I was going to do multifamily real estate, then I was going to be gung ho and all in so that I could help as many others as possible. And I like to think that's what makes me different from others in this industry—I put the investors first and work my ass off for them because they're my top priority.

Once I made that decision, everything started to line up. I had Prostoig Capital up and running, and by January 2020, I had three deals lined up, and everything was rocking and rolling. Things were looking great.

Then COVID-19 hit. I had a deal go sour. A second one got sidelined, but then one of them continued. It's March 2020 now, and when everything shuts down, that includes my dental office, so I'm not seeing patients. But then I got a pleasant surprise in April. My distributions continued because people were actually paying their rent. My stock portfolios all crashed, but thankfully I'd already liquidated my bonds because I knew something bad was coming. I just didn't know what exactly.

In July the sidelined deal finally went through, and so I felt super pumped because here I had revenue and earnings coming in even though I didn't have patients coming into the office yet. Then I contacted a guy, who's now become a good friend, and ended up doing the biggest deal yet—a three-hundred-plus unit that I was also able to get some other friends to jump on board with and invest in with us.

All of that really got the ball rolling, as more deals came along and more people jumped on board. Then I asked myself, "Why am I relying on other people to do the main syndications? I should start taking this on myself." So at the beginning of 2021, I took the lead on a forty-unit deal with three other partners in North Carolina so that I could learn the final pieces of the process that I'd never been involved in.

PART TWO

How It All Works

Before we get into how all this works, I want you to know this book isn't here to convince you to copy what I've done. You can start with being a passive investor and stop there if you want. Because I know firsthand how difficult it is to be a dentist and manage all the things that have to be done, I also know this isn't going to be everyone's cup of tea.

The beauty is that you don't have to know everything in the beginning, and you don't have to be a genius to do this. Believe me. So I'm going to lay out some of the vocabulary and concepts in the multifamily real estate industry so you can take some easy baby steps. Whether you decide to invest in it for yourself or not, I hope that by introducing you to the basics, I can at least clear up some misconceptions and help you overcome the fears around investing in real estate— which is why at Prostoig Capital I've designed things around a people-first mindset.

A People-First Approach

Who are the people? The investors and residents, of course—but we'll talk about these two groups separately to keep things simple.

Part of the investor-first approach is making sure that the property investors know exactly where the money is going since they are giving me so much trust and control in the process. And since I learned that you can't do this on your own, I've since put together a team of people to keep things moving smoothly. That's exactly what I'm here for—putting in the legwork and making the deals happen so that you don't have to.

You might be asking, "But what if I want to go out and do this myself? Why should I invest in your deals when I could go out and make my own?" Well, actually, you could. But it does take a lot of time and work; I think trying to do both is a huge mistake. So if you're ready to leave dentistry and do this full time, be my guest. But if you're looking to grow wealth passively while continuing your practice, then that's where I can absolutely be an asset to you.

As you see that passive income grow, you can also feel good about it too. I've learned that in multifamily real estate, the deals often involve people who aren't very happy with the current situation—living in run-down apartments overseen by "slumlords" or heartless corporations that couldn't care less about the conditions or whether the management is treating them well.

But first I want to go back to something I mentioned earlier: risk. There's always risk in every kind of investment. The stock market can go down, which can cause your 401(k) to drop, but generally, you don't really think about that because you know it'll go back up over time. You just hope that doesn't happen at the wrong point of your career when you actually need the 401(k) for what it was designed for. There's also risk in investing in individual stocks, because sometimes those companies go out of business, and then those shares lose all their value. People forget that.

So yes, there's risk in real estate investing too. Some people like to point to 2008 and say, "See, that's why I don't want to get into real estate." But people seem to forget that the Great Recession was caused by a crash in subprime mortgages—which is a different ball game than multifamily-unit properties. In my experience, those stay a lot steadier in terms of cash flow.

Still, can a deal go sour and you lose your money? Sure. But it can also go great, and you see your money double or triple from it. In my experience, the breakeven on these deals has been better than in the market. Plus, there's a greater safety net with real estate investing. For one thing, if you lose money on a deal, it's a pretty easy tax write-off compared to writing off losses in the stock market. But also, if you lose money in the market, the government won't do a thing to help you out, whereas with the housing market, they have an interest in protecting it. That's why during the COVID-19 pandemic, the federal government offered things like rental assistance.

Before I learned all this, one of my biggest misconceptions was that I saw all these different investments as essentially equal—now I know better. Back then, I didn't view a loss in the stock market as a realized loss, but now I do because even when the market goes back up, I still lost that money and didn't get anything in return.

Another misconception that a lot of people have when looking at real estate is looking at debt as a liability. But actually what I've learned is that debt can be an asset. How? Well, because even if you're paying interest of 4 to 6 percent, you're still below inflation, which means you're actually making money on the debt due to the difference between the two rates.

> **If you're paying interest of 4 to 6 percent, you're still below inflation.**

Also, the debt becomes an asset because you're not paying the debt by yourself. Ultimately, it's the residents who are paying for it in the form of rent. So these two things combined make the debt a double asset for you. This reasoning can be applied to all aspects of owning the property. For example, when the roof needs to be replaced, yes, it sucks at the time because I have to front some money, but over time, the rents pay for the repair.

Finally, I don't think you should put all of your money into this. Okay? I don't think that would be wise at all! I'm a big believer in it myself, of course, so I wouldn't mind doing that, but I don't think everybody should. This is about diversifying where your money is and having more options to see it grow. I think putting 10 to 25 percent of your investments into this is completely reasonable while also keeping things like 401(k)s, stocks, bonds, etc., all in play. But I'm not a financial advisor, so I think you should speak to your advisor about your specific situation first.

In other words, I'm not here to talk you into anything you don't want to do. I myself had a lot of fears about investing in real estate when I first started because I had a lot of misconceptions about how it all worked. And I wasn't hurting for money—I just wanted to be a good steward of what I had and grow it for the sake of my loved ones. But I was so fed up with the status quo of investing that it helped me overcome those fears and try something new. And I'm so glad I did.

Now, for the resident's part of the people-first approach, that's the part of this that really motivates me and gives me a sense of purpose. When I was throwing money at the stock market, chasing numbers, who was I really helping at the end of the day? I was making a few bucks here and there for myself, yeah, but I was really just helping out the Wall Street guys and big banks make more money.

When a property changes hands, for the first six months to a year, the residents might not even realize it. So when I go visit one of my properties, I never tell anyone there that I'm the new owner. I always say I'm an inspector or contractor so that I can get transparent feedback. They'll complain to me, "The owner of this place is really cheap."

And I'll say, "Why do you say that?"

And from there, they'll give me a ton of information about what kind of problems need to be fixed that I would never get out of them if they knew who I really was. I've had residents smoke weed in front of me or throw trash on the ground—and that's actually what I want to see, because it shows me what the culture of the place is like and, well, which residents are really good and have valid feedback and which ones probably need to go.

I say all this to point out that the investment you make in these properties isn't just about reaping the long-term financial rewards; it's also about making them a better place for people to live, for however long they are there. When we go into a property, our goal is to always improve the experience for the people who live there. If we're going to be taking their rent money, we better be making sure that we're making it worth it and providing them value! Everyone deserves to have a safe place to call home. It makes them better members of society, better patients, and better residents. So it really ends up being a win-win for everybody.

I'm not in the slumlord business, and on the occasions when we decide to sell a property that we've been invested in, we sure as hell better leave it in a better place than when we found it. Not only is it the right ethical thing to do to make sure they're happy and taken care of, but it's the right business thing too—because if we don't take care of them, then they'll pack up and go somewhere else, and that's lost revenue.

A lot of us grew up with the myth that you can either do good for people or make money but that the two things can't mix. But in multifamily investing, these ideas are not only mixed but married! I believe if you give people a great place to live, they'll stick around longer, they'll refer their friends and family to live there, and it's better for everyone. It's beautiful, really, and it makes you feel a ton better about where you're putting your money, even as you grow it.

Multifamily investing has given so much to me: from growing my wealth, to providing for my family, to giving me a sense of purpose and mission that I can feel good about. But another thing it's given me, which I didn't even realize I was looking for, is freedom with my time. Yes, I still have to give time to it, but it's more on my terms, allowing me to be more present for my family and to find the lifestyle I was looking for all along.

There's really nothing that original or unique about what I've done. I've just tried to make sure that I keep people first in everything. If that makes me unique, then so be it. But now let's get to the real meat of the conversation: How exactly does it all work?

The Basics

How do you actually make money off of all this? Well, the math behind it is so simple it's almost ridiculous—

revenue from rent money and other income – expenses – bank payments = cash flow

—which is then divided up between investors and general partners, based on their contributions. And then you follow that same pattern each month that goes by so that you're generating income each month and each year. Or you get a payout when the property is sold, if that ever happens.

There is a bit more complicated math that plays into it, and we'll quickly talk about some of those factors because I like being transparent with people from the beginning. So let's get into some of those terms real quick.

CASH ON CASH

For a passive investor, *cash on cash* is one of the most important and powerful metrics to look at because it's based on the returns you're getting *right now* from the money you put in. I'm going to keep it real simple here, but there are two sides of the coin:

1. What the rents are producing in monthly revenue, as seen in the equation above.

2. The enhanced appreciation on what you've invested.

So let's say that you've invested $100,000 into a property and that cash on cash for the deal is 6 percent—meaning that every year you should be seeing $6,000 total, usually paid out in quarterly (or sometimes monthly) installments. The reason this is so powerful is because you usually see it go up as time goes on—that's when the real magic happens.

That's because during the first couple of years, you might be starting with leases that are under market value. But over time, when you're not having to do major upgrades but only regular maintenance and you're able to justify bumping the rents up to market value, that translates into greater return— that is, the *enhanced appreciation* side of things.

Furthermore, since we take out bank loans to purchase these properties, there's a good chance we do a refinance at some point—so when we pull out some of the equity, that means increasing the returns on your funds still in the deal. When you invest in multifamily real estate, you're doing it for the long haul, not a quick turnaround. So you might have zero cash on cash return in the first couple of years, but then the dividends start kicking in once rent starts to outweigh expenses and refinances take place. So it's an important metric to consider for a property so that there are no surprises about why you're not getting a ton of return in the beginning if the property needed a ton of work. It's not the same across all deals, so you need to be able to go through the deal with a fine-tooth comb and know what your expectations should be—which is part of what I do for potential investors.

Generally, I'm looking at properties that will net somewhere in the neighborhood of 6 to 10 percent cash on cash. So let's say the deal I'm looking at is 8 percent. That means I'm getting 2 percent each quarter. If I've invested $100,000, that's $2,000 a quarter I can expect—which might be tax free, by the way—but you'll need to talk to your tax professional about that since tax implications will vary person to person obviously.

Now, let's say in year three, we do the refinance, and instead of the $100,000 that I initially invested, there's $50,000 left in there. The cash on cash might actually go up to as much as 12 or 15 percent (or even more!) because of the lower total return. And now you get back the $50,000 from the initial investment, which you can turn around and invest in another deal if you want to—which is better than compounding because you're creating exponential growth from your investment. Part of the power of this is that we own the property but with none of our own money actually in it because we're using the bank's money. And being able to take out part of that initial investment and pursue another deal is just part of how you continue to generate wealth.

INTERNAL RATE OF RETURN

Internal rate of return (IRR) is the next metric that can be really powerful to look at when comparing deals, but it can be confusing for people because it's a complicated formula. And I don't want to turn this into a math textbook.

At its simplest, IRR is just an analysis to estimate how profitable a potential investment can be for you. So if cash on cash looks at what you're taking home as mailbox money *right now*, then IRR looks at what you're making *in the future* based on the value of the dollar now. There are three main numbers used to calculate it:

1. Cash flow at the current time.

2. The IRR, which is a discount rate of the return expressed as a decimal value.

3. The time period of the investment.

Think of it like this: If I go buy an Americano coffee today, it's going to cost me four or five dollars, but three years from now, it might be seven or eight dollars. So IRR takes this increase into consideration—the cost of the net present value of what the dollar is worth now compared to what it may be worth in the future.

Bringing this back down to the investments then, who cares if you technically make $10,000 on a property if the dollar value has changed to the point where it's actually worth less than what you put into it? IRR helps us avoid that scenario, so I'm typically looking at deals with projected 13 to 16 percent IRR because it's helping me gauge the risk of the deal. If it gets up to 25 percent, that's when it could be a riskier deal, but you also have to know the story behind the number and weigh the time of the deal that you're looking at.

For example, let's say you have higher cash on cash returns in the beginning of a deal or refinance early or have a quick sale, then you're going to have a higher IRR—no problem. If you're holding it for a shorter period of time, that 25 percent IRR isn't so scary because it's a quicker transaction. But if you have a ten-year hold on a deal, you'll want to see that 13 to 16 percent IRR.

So this is why we try to hold on to properties for longer at Prostoig Capital LLC, because in years zero to three of owning a property, you are creating a lot of value to the residents, which in turn creates a *huge* increase in value to the property itself. This allows us to increase the bottom line (the rents), which increases cash flow. Once that cash flow is there, we obviously want to take advantage of it as long as possible.

> **You are creating a lot of value to the residents, which in turn creates a huge increase in value to the property itself.**

Another reason we hold on to properties for so long is the taxes. The US government actually wants you to hold on to these properties for a long time because you're creating a business, creating housing, and providing jobs—all the things they want you to do. So they incentivize you holding on to those properties because when you sell, they're going to want to recapture as much from you as possible, and you'll get hit harder on your taxes, maybe even jumping up a tax bracket if you're a high net worth individual. So we try not to sell. But even when we do, there are ways around those taxes—such as the *1031 exchange*, where you transfer your investment into another syndication and use the depreciation to offset some of the taxes on the sale. But that's another thing that I would help walk you through at the appropriate time.

To go back to what I was saying earlier about taking care of our tenants, that's why we want to create tremendous value for them, because we know a lot of money and work is going to be spent in those first couple of years when we might have a lower cash on cash return—if any—but we are building up the IRR for the future. But they will be willing to stick around and pay the increase in rent because of the value being provided, and you'll be able to attract new people who appreciate the value.

AVERAGE ANNUAL RETURN

Don't worry. This one's pretty easy. *Average annual return* (AAR) is simply a number that explains how much of a return you would get without including the net present value of the dollar. So if you buy an apartment building for $100,000 today in cash and then sell it for $200,000 in five years, that's $100,000 gained over five years, which comes out to $20,000 a year or a 20 percent annualized return. Your AAR is usually going to be a higher percentage rate than your IRR, but it's just another number to consider when looking at deals.

Quick high-level investing tip for you: many fund managers and financial advisors will use this tool to make you appear to get higher returns, which is why I like IRR better for evaluating a deal. For example, if your financial manager tells you that over the last few years, you had a 25 percent AAR, it would sound great, right? Maybe, but it depends. Let's say you invested $100,000 with this manager two years ago, and the first year you got a negative 50 percent return, so you were left with $50,000. The next year you got a whopping 100 percent return, so now you are back to your original $100,000. Therefore, it was truly a 0 percent return. But AAR would be calculated –50% + 100% = 50% for the total annualized return, then divided by the amount of time (two years), and you arrive at that 25 percent AAR.

In other words, it's important to know the story *behind* the numbers, not the numbers alone!

CAPITALIZATION RATE

Capitalization rate (cap rate) is a term that gets used a lot in commercial real estate, but all it means is the income you get on the property, without taking into consideration the debt service, divided by the current value of the property (or the purchase price of the property):

net operating income / value of property = cap rate

The reason this gets talked about a lot is due to how the purchase price, refinance price, or sales price of the property can be manipulated. There are a couple of ways you can consider the cap rate in an area: (1) you can ask brokers in the area about the value, or (2) you can look it up online to see the value. Cap rate is also based on the type and class of property.

We'll talk about this concept of property class in the next section, but to keep it simple: the higher the class of the property, the lower the cap rate. That usually requires a lower-class property because this makes it a riskier property but with more potential.

Let's say you pay cash for a property that's $100,000 with a 5 percent cap rate, then you would expect a $5,000 return on it. But just like with IRR, you need to know the story behind the rate that the broker is telling you. What does that 5 percent really mean? What's the class of the property? What is the area it's in like? Again, this is part of what I do, assessing the story behind that number, not just looking at the number.

Realistically, I shoot for a cap rate close to 6 percent. That can be almost impossible, but it helps me narrow down the deals I look at, and on a practical level, this helps me find my target properties: the worst properties in the best areas.

The Process

To understand the process, we're going to start with understanding the properties themselves because they're what you're putting your money into at the end of the day. As I mentioned above, I look for the worst properties in the best areas. What does that mean?

There are four standard classes of properties used in the industry: A, B, C, and D. For practical reasons, we'll cover them in reverse order.

D CLASS

This is the type of property where you're not going to be comfortable walking around at night. It's what you would think of as the slums, with poverty-level tenants, not really the ideal properties we're going after because they're usually also located in bad areas.

C CLASS

This could be thought of as a fixer-upper type. It's a bit run down, and the people living there are mostly going to be working class. You'd be okay walking around at night, but there won't be any fancy appliances.

B CLASS

The B class properties are where you're going to find renters who are in middle management, so you'll see upgraded amenities, like stainless steel appliances, granite countertops, covered parking, good landscaping, and such.

A CLASS

Obviously, this is the top tier, where you're finding places that could rival the nicest homes in the area in terms of their interiors and amenities. High-end everything. The tenants here are probably earning six figures plus.

The reason I primarily go after C class properties is because you can find them in nice areas. They just need some work. When I'm scouting a new deal, I'll look at areas that have an Apple store—or a Starbucks because, while I don't care for their coffee personally, I know if there's a Starbucks in the area, there are people in the area who can afford it.

If I can acquire a C class property at a good price, fix it up, and bring it up to a B, then suddenly other people want to live there, and word gets out. This will also allow us to justify raising the rents over time, increasing the returns and the value of the property as a whole for whenever we refinance or if we ever decide to sell. And meanwhile, we're improving the living situation for the people living there by fixing it up, bringing in better management, listening to what they want, and making it a place where they want to stay. It's pretty straightforward.

I won't say I'll never invest in a higher-class property like a B or even an A. There are times to do so and passive investors who want to do so. These can be really consistent properties to hold on to, but in terms of creating value and generating wealth, you get the biggest bang for your buck from buying the C class properties and bringing them up to a B class.

THE SYNDICATION MODEL

Once I've found a deal that looks promising and want to move forward on purchasing the property, the next steps that are taken go through a process known as *syndication*. Basically, it means that there will be a series of legal documents that need to be signed indicating whether you're a *general partner* (GP) on the deal, a *limited partner* (LP), or both.

The first document is called a *private placement memorandum* (PPM), which is something that the lawyers come up with to disclose all the risks of the investment and how exactly the disinvestment is going to run. It also addresses the real estate in general, any of the information that we have passed on to them from our own research of the property.

This is done once we have a property under contract. So one thing that's really important to understand here that's different from other types of investing is that you're not actually buying the property itself with the money you invest—you're actually buying shares of the company that owns the property.

The other main document is the *limited partnership agreement*, which is the legal contract between the GPs who are serving as the syndicators and the LPs who are serving as the investors. This just makes sure everyone's on the same page by outlining everyone's roles and responsibilities as well as spelling out how the shares work.

If you're an LP, there's also a *subscription agreement*, where you're telling the syndicator or GP that you qualify to take part in the investment. It will spell out the details for the transaction you're going to make: how many shares you're buying, the price of those shares, and some other fun legal items, like confidentiality agreements. Again, nothing too scary here, just one of those things that is good to have for documentation so you don't run into problems later on. As much as I love a good handshake or verbal promise, trust me, you want everything in writing, too, especially when you're talking about the amounts of money that are involved here.

TYPES OF INVESTORS

The types of investors that I'm looking to invest passively in these deals are my friends, friends of friends, or family. So if you're reading this right now, I already count you in one of those categories right off the bat.

For one thing, this makes the process a lot cleaner because a lot of the deals that I do are what's known as a *506(b) syndication*. For another thing, with our investor-first approach, I want to work with people I trust and who trust me. I just think that's good common sense.

Another benefit of 506(b) is that you don't have to be accredited. It's great for you to have some knowledge of investing—and that's part of why I wanted to write this book—but what's most important is that it's people I know and trust and want to join me in the success I've had.

A key thing to know about 506(b) is that because it's restricted to friends and family, you can't advertise it in any shape or form. I can't go on social media and say, "Hey, guys. I've got this great deal happening. Go check out my website!" That's a huge no-no that's going to get the SEC coming after you, and you don't want that!

There's also such a thing as a 506(c) that allows unlimited investors, and they can be anyone. I could walk into a coffee shop, walk up to a stranger, and say, "Hey, I've got a great investment if you're interested in 15 percent annual returns." Or I could post it for the whole world to see online. But I'll only be able to take *accredited investors*. To qualify for that, you have to make $200,000 a year if single or $300,000 a year combined if married, or you must have a net worth of $1 million, excluding the value of your primary home.

The big takeaway for all this, though, is that part of why I love this industry so much is that I get to help people become passive investors and walk through this process. I've already done the hard parts, and these pieces exist to put on paper the trust that's already been built up and make sure that you're a part of the deals that you want to be a part of. Not every deal is going to be for you. That's all right. Not every deal is for me either. That's why I spend my time doing the heavy lifting of the research and number crunching.

And I'd be lying through my teeth to make you think I do this alone. The fact of the matter is, for all this to work, you need a great team to support the process so that everyone's happy—me, you, the bank, and anyone else being served in the process.

Who Do You Need?

So let's chat a bit here about the team that needs to be assembled to make multifamily investing work. But first, I want to make something really clear: *you* don't have to assemble this team—I've already done it! Of course, if you want to go out and build your own real estate company, then the following list will be a great place for you to start seeing what you need to do. But if you want to be a passive investor, then this list will be great for showing you what kinds of things are going on behind the scenes.

I've learned that the first person you need to make all this work is the transaction attorney. When I was assembling my team, I was fortunate enough to have a rock star syndication attorney who was also a transaction attorney.

It's also key to have a kick-ass real estate broker who likes you. Not only will they be key in helping you find great properties, but they're great for building your network. In fact, it was my broker who turned out to be the biggest help in my search for a property manager when the time came for one.

This might come as a surprise, but the biggest financial investor is actually the bank. They are investing anywhere from 50- to 80-plus percent of the capital, which means they are a partner and should be treated as such. I can't say enough how important it is to have multiple great relationships with banks.

Speaking of, your property manager is the biggest piece of this puzzle. If you look at the big scheme of things, this is the person who makes or breaks everything. Thankfully, I've got one whose attitude is "Hey, man, I got you," and he just wants to take care of me and help the business grow. In fact, he even keeps me up to date on things like any changes with real estate taxes, which very few property managers can do. And more importantly than all of that is how he interacts with his staff.

Your property manager is the biggest piece of this puzzle.

After I bought the property, he let me observe his interactions with staff and even explained to me how the leasing office and the leases work, which is pretty rare in the world of property management. He's so essential to things that I've even got him on the board for the apartment complex.

Property management is your ground level in the whole venture, the most important thing for these apartments to not only operate well but to care for people. If you've got a bad property manager, the game's over. But if they're taking care of the residents—who call about a leak in their apartment, and it gets taken care of quickly—then everything else falls into place.

Yeah, residents will be upset when there's a rent increase, but if you're taking care of them and things are working well, then they'll still stick around. But if you don't take care of the property, even if you keep the rents the same, things will fall through, and people will move on, taking their rent with them.

So having a great relationship with the property manager can really be the difference between success and failure. While I do a lot of work on the front end of the deal, once that's done, it's the property management company that bears the biggest load—that's what we pay them for. There will be hard conversations at times—talking about bills and expenses and whatever else comes along, too—but just like any relationship, building trust is crucial.

I like to approach things with an abundance mindset in how I interact with all of these individuals, but especially the property manager. I've known others in this industry who make assumptions about property managers ripping them off, so it creates mistrust between you and them. I'm not naive about that kind of stuff—I know it can happen, sure—but treating people well goes a long, long way in preventing it from happening.

The Rules and Advantages

Now, I know what you're thinking because I thought it too: "Can't I make more money from being a dentist?" Well, of course! But that's why you're not doing this as a full-time job and also why it's a form of investment, not a side hustle. You can literally just invest, let others do the bulk of the work, and then have the regular earnings come in each month.

So as we wrap up here, there are a few basic rules I want you to think about to decide if this is for you—or not.

RULE NUMBER ONE: NOT ALL REAL ESTATE INVESTING IS CREATED EQUAL

Multifamily investing isn't the same as renting out a single-family dwelling or a vacation home. That's why it's so important to understand the types of properties, the areas they're located in, what the IRR numbers mean, and so on. If you come on this journey with me, there will be ample oppor-

INVESTING IN LIFE

tunity for more discussion. If you're confused by something, just ask! That's exactly how I learned.

Some might ask, "If I've got the money for it, why not just do this myself and go buy some houses and rent them out?" That's great if that's what you want to do. It requires more work on your part, but for those who want to be more hands-on, it might be a better option. As a reminder, with the size of our deals, we get a lot of help from the banks if there's a crisis because they've put their money in it too. They care less about a few rental houses and will be less helpful.

RULE NUMBER TWO: DON'T DABBLE IN REAL ESTATE—GET EDUCATED!

Imagine if you tried to dabble in dentistry without any training. It's not going to go well for anyone! Same thing here. Dabbling with real estate while running your office takes up time and focus that you probably don't have.

One thing I like to be up front about is that when you become part of a syndicate, even as a passive investor, you're a partner in the deal now. So if someone comes to me and says, "Hey David, I want to get out; I want to dissolve my membership," it's not as easy as just handing back their share of the money.

I mentioned before we have our own syndication attorney, and dissolving membership is going to require fees that could be anywhere from $1,000 to $5,000—and then you also have to find another partner willing to buy your shares and figure out a fair price for it. Obviously, we understand things can

54

change for people, and maybe a crisis happens, sure. While you don't have to be involved in the day-to-day operation of things, you're still making a long-term commitment.

I know that scares some people, and that's all right— maybe that means it's not for you. But what I find exciting is the process of creating equity and generational wealth for you!

RULE NUMBER THREE: FOCUS ON GENERATIONAL WEALTH

Don't expect to be able to quit your job and just sit back on what you get on your returns, at least not initially. While you'll certainly get returns and cash flow that you can use at your discretion, I find it's best to think of this as a way to create generational wealth, something you'll be able to pass down to your kids and grandkids to help them out. You can literally double your money in five years and quadruple it in ten if you do this, so think about what that could do for your family and the generations you might never see. You can't take it with you, but you can make a huge impact.

If you can accept and live by those rules, then you get to enjoy some of the advantages we haven't touched on yet.

ADVANTAGE NUMBER ONE: YOU CAN DO THIS FROM ANYWHERE IN THE US

Actually, I've even had a couple of foreign investors join in. People sometimes think that getting into real estate means being bound by geography, but I've had deals all over the country, which gives great leverage to finding the best opportunities.

ADVANTAGE NUMBER TWO: YOU'RE NOT DOING IT ALONE

This is something you do with others just like you. There's safety in numbers—it reduces risk, generates confidence in the process, and gives you a built-in community to celebrate with when the returns start coming in.

ADVANTAGE NUMBER THREE: IT DOESN'T HAVE TO RULE OVER YOUR LIFE

You can be a passive investor and still run your dental or medical office. You don't have to stress about missing out on a trade. Once the initial paperwork is done and your portion is transferred, you can largely take a back seat if you choose.

Yes, you're committed and in the car for the ride, but you're not driving the car—you just sit back and enjoy the view. Or, like me, you can choose to get as involved as you like, stepping into the passenger's seat or even the driver's seat, and go find your own deals if you want to. The key thing is that it doesn't own you.

Now What?

The ball's in your court. By now, you probably have at least some notion of whether this is for you or not. If not, then I appreciate you at least taking the time to learn about what I do. I don't expect it to be for everyone! But if the idea of this intrigues or excites you, then let's talk. If you still have questions or need to go deeper than what we could do here, great—let's talk.

You can reach out to me through our website, prostoig.com, or even email me at dsi@prostoig.com. Or you know what? Just give me a call if you want at (610) 609-1396.

I don't get tired talking about this, believe me, so if you want to learn more, I'm ready to continue the conversation when you're ready!

Notes

Notes

CPSIA information can be obtained
at www.ICGtesting.com
Printed in the USA
BVHW042206151122
652066BV00003B/51

9 781642 253979